TREASURE HUNTERS

THE SEARCH FOR

GOLD

KLONDIKE
GOLD

CALIFORNIA
GOLD

OAK ISLAND
TREASURE

BLACKBEARD'S TREASURE ?

CAPTAIN KIDD'S TREASURE ?

AZTEC
GOLD

ATLANTIC
OCEAN

BUCCANEER
TERRITORY

THE TREASURE OF
THE *MARY DEARE*

EL DORADO ?

DRAKE'S
TREASURE

INCA
GOLD

THE PANAGYURISHTE
TREASURE

THE GOLDEN
HELMET OF UR

THE OXUS
TREASURE

PACIFIC
OCEAN

THE GOLDEN
HEAD OF GHANA

EL MINA

INDIAN
OCEAN

TRANSVAAL
GOLD

BLUE MOUNTAIN
GOLD

TREASURE HUNTERS

THE SEARCH FOR

GOLD

NICOLA BARBER

RSVP

RAINTREE
STECK-VAUGHN
PUBLISHERS
The Steck-Vaughn Company

Austin, Texas

TREASURE HUNTERS

This book is dedicated to Finlay

Published by Raintree Steck-Vaughn Publishers, an imprint of Steck-Vaughn
Company

Concept Designer: Jane Hannath
Designer and Typesetter: Kudos
Illustrator: Mike White
Commissioning Editor: Fiona Courtenay-Thompson
Editors: Lisa Edwards, William P. Mara
Copy Editor: Diana Russell

Photograph Acknowledgments: AKG London p17(tl), 18(cb), 19(ct); Ancient Art &
Architecture Collection 12(br), 13(cr), 20(cl), 24(tr), 28(cl), 41(bl); C M Dixon p11(tr);
e.t. archive p18(tr), 25(c), 36(bl), 37(t); Mary Evans Picture Library p 27(tl), 33(tr),
38(bl), 43(tr); Rex Features p 23(bl), 31(ct); Ann Ronan at Image Select p 8(cr), 32(tr),
35(bl); Werner Forman Archive p14(cl), 15(br).

Picture research: Image Select, London

Library of Congress Cataloging-in-Publication Data

Barber, Nicola.
     The search for gold / Nicola Barber.
        p.   cm. — (Treasure hunters)
     Includes bibliographical references and index.
     Summary: Surveys the activities of the explorers and pirates who
went in search of gold and describes the unsolved mysteries of lost
treasures of the world.
     ISBN 0-8172-4837-4
     1. Treasure-trove—Juvenile literature.   [1. Buried treasure.]
I. Title.   II. Series: Treasure hunters (Austin, Tex.)
G525.B2616   1998
904—dc21   96-37564
                                                 CIP
                                                 AC

Printed in Hong Kong by Wing King Tong
1 2 3 4 5 6 7 8 9 HK 01 00 99 98 97

Map artwork on pp. 2–3 by Bruce Hogarth

CONTENTS

INTRODUCTION

What precious metal has led people to go into battle, to leave their homes and travel to the other side of the world, to spend years searching for the truth behind the vaguest rumors, even to commit murder? The answer is gold. In this book, we look at the stories of treasure hunters throughout the ages who have gone in search of gold.

Gold was one of the first metals to be worked by humans, and from the earliest times people have loved its glowing, yellow color. Gold is a soft metal, so it is easy to hammer and shape in its natural form. A few ounces of it can be drawn out into a wire many miles long, or beaten flat into a thin sheet of gold leaf many feet square.

Gold is almost indestructible. It is not affected by sunlight, fire, or seawater; it doesn't become tarnished like silver or corroded like iron. Gold objects brought up from the seabed, or found buried deep in the ground, can be as bright and gold-colored as when they were first made. It takes a fire of incredible heat to melt gold: 1945° Fahrenheit (1063°C). Compare this to the melting point of lead 620°F (327°C) or tin 448°F (231°C).

One of the reasons gold is so durable is that it reacts with very few other chemicals or gases. Gold is so long-lasting and so valuable that it is used over and over again. It's strange to think that some of the gold in the ring on your finger could perhaps originally have come from the great Inca Empire in South America (see page 18).

A beautiful Egyptian mask inlaid with gold.

Taken from an ancient Egyptian tomb painting, this scene shows workmen heating and pouring gold.

8

Golden myths

Gold is beautiful, enduring, and unchanging. It is not surprising that it has always been used by humans to glorify their gods and to adorn their kings and queens. Because of its color, gold has also long been associated with the sun. The ancient Egyptians believed that their sun god, Ra, was born each morning as a calf, became a powerful bull at midday, and turned to gold as the sun set each evening.

There are many stories from all over the world about gold and the effect it has upon people. One of the most famous is the Greek legend of King Midas. In return for a favor to a god, Midas was offered anything in the world. He asked that all he touched should immediately turn to gold. After transforming most of the objects in his palace into solid gold, Midas started to get hungry. But as soon as he touched the delicious spread placed before him, the food became gold. Worse, his daughter rushed in to greet him and, before he could stop her, she embraced him—only to be turned instantly into a golden statue. A wiser man, Midas begged to be released from this curse. Eventually the story ends happily, but this is a cautionary tale about the ability of gold to corrupt people's minds. We will learn much more about the powerful lure of gold throughout the rest of this book.

King Midas turned everything that he touched to gold.

GOLDEN WORDS

There are many words and phrases that include the word "gold." Some, such as "golden retriever," "golden eagle," or "goldfish," refer to its color. Others, such as "gold medal" or "gold star," use the idea of gold as something very valuable to show that someone has reached the highest grade. How many other golden associations can you think of?
Here are just a few more:

- ★ the pot of gold
- ★ the Golden Gate Bridge
- ★ Goldilocks
- ★ the Golden Rule
- ★ golden anniversary
- ★ "as good as gold"

GOLD: LOST AND FOUND

How many treasure hoards are there scattered around the world? In underground tombs, buried chests, and wrecks far below the waves, golden treasure lies dark and hidden. Here are the stories of just a few of the riches of the past that have been discovered, including the tale of how the treasure of the Oxus was found—and then nearly lost again.

In 1877 a hoard of gold objects was found on the banks of the Oxus River (now known as the Anu Darya), which marks the border between Afghanistan and the countries to the north. No one knows exactly where the hoard was discovered or who found it. Today you can see many of the Oxus treasures in the British Museum in London, but there were several adventures before they finally got there.

Skirmish in the Khyber Pass

Three years after the discovery of the hoard, the Oxus gold was in the hands of three merchants and their servant as they made their way along the steep, rocky paths of the Khyber Pass. Plodding behind them came several mules, carrying saddlebags laden with precious jewelry and ornaments. The merchants were taking their treasures to sell in Rawalpindi, in present-day Pakistan.

The merchants knew the danger of their journey, particularly with such a rich cargo. At one of the loneliest places in the pass, their worst fears came true. Suddenly they were surrounded by well-armed brigands, who quickly overpowered the merchants.

The brigands fight over their loot.

The brigands forced the merchants and their servant to march into the mountains, leading their mules, until they reached some caves hidden in a remote spot. Here, the robbers intended to divide up the loot.

Escape!

The brigands ordered the merchants to start unloading their mules, greedily watching every move. But they were so intent on their newfound wealth that they completely forgot about the merchants' servant. Seeing his chance, the servant slipped quietly away, running as fast as he could back to the road and on to a British army camp nearby.

Gasping with fear and exhaustion, the servant told his story to Captain Francis Burton, one of the officers in the camp. Immediately Burton set out for the brigands' hideout, accompanied by two soldiers. When he reached the caves, just before midnight, a strange sight met his eyes. There were the three merchants, now tied up and terrified. The treasure was spread out all over the floor of the cave, glittering in the firelight. Several of the brigands were arguing loudly

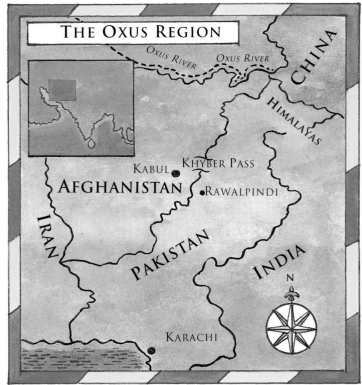

No one knows exactly where the Oxus treasure was found, but it was probably on the banks of the Oxus River in northern Afghanistan.

over who should get what, and several more were lying groaning on the floor, injured after fighting over their precious loot.

PERSIAN GOLD

Where did the fabulous gold jewelry and ornaments of the Oxus treasure come from, and who made them? Most of the pieces probably date from between 500 and 300 BC. They were made by people from the ancient Persian Empire, which once spread from Egypt to India. The treasure includes gold armlets and rings, dishes and bowls, and tiny golden trinkets. One of the most famous pieces is a small model of a chariot drawn by four horses.

A miniature chariot, part of the Oxus treasure. Inside the chariot, a Persian prince sits on a long seat facing sideways.

11

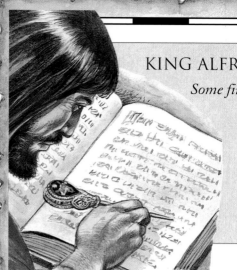

The gold is recovered

Captain Burton decided to negotiate with the brigands, and before long they agreed to hand over the merchants and a large part of the treasure. Burton then set off on the journey back to the camp. At least that is what he told the brigands he was about to do. In reality, he and the merchants spent the rest of the night in hiding, because he guessed that the only reason the robbers had returned the treasure so readily was that they were already plotting to spring another attack, and this time they would kill both him and the merchants.

At six o'clock the next morning, Captain Burton, his soldiers, the merchants, and the heavily laden mules finally reached the safety of the British camp. A warning was sent to the brigands that unless they gave up the rest of the gold, a large force would be sent to fight them. In the end about three-quarters of it was recovered; the rest was probably hidden or melted down.

And afterward . . .

The merchants went on to sell the treasure to dealers in Rawalpindi. Much of it was eventually bought by General Sir Alexander Cunningham, and then by Sir Augustus Wollaston Franks, who gave it to the British Museum. The museum now has about 180 pieces belonging to the Oxus treasure. But many experts believe that not all the pieces belong to the original hoard and that some were added by dealers.

THE PANAGYURISHTE TREASURE

The story of the Panagyurishte treasure is a tale of a fabulous golden hoard found entirely by chance. Panagyurishte is a small town in Bulgaria. One day in 1949, three workmen were digging in a field just outside the town when one of them noticed something glittering in the newly turned soil. They dug deeper and, to their astonishment, unearthed an amazing collection of goblets, bowls, and jugs, all made from solid gold. Some of the vessels in the hoard were made in the shapes of animals' heads, like the one here.

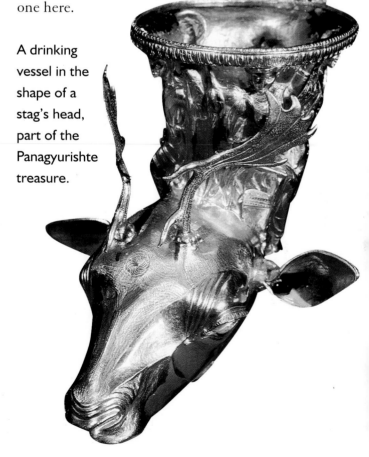

A drinking vessel in the shape of a stag's head, part of the Panagyurishte treasure.

Who did the treasure originally belong to? Why was it buried in the middle of a field? No one knows the answers to these questions.

What we do know is that the area around Panagyurishte was once part of Thrace, a land that lay to the north of ancient Greece. Its people were noted for their bravery and skill in battle, but Thrace was invaded around 350 BC by fierce peoples from the north. Perhaps these valuable drinking vessels were hurriedly buried by a Thracian nobleman as he was forced by the invaders to flee. But we will never know for sure.

THE GOLDEN HELMET OF UR

The British archaeologist Sir Leonard Woolley unearthed many golden treasures in his excavations at Ur. The site of this ancient city lies in Iraq, halfway between Baghdad and the head of the Persian Gulf. About 4,000 years ago, Ur was one of the most important cities in this region. In one of the royal tombs, Woolley found the body of a prince called Meskalamdug. On his head was a helmet of beaten gold in the shape of a wig, with the hair knotted into a neat bun at the back. Around the edge of the helmet were lace holes for the padding that the prince wore underneath.

The golden helmet of Meskalamdug.

Three workmen dug up the fabulous Panagyurishte treasure by chance. Some of the vessels they found took the shape of animals' and women's heads. These were modeled after the gods and heroes of ancient Greek myths.

THE AFRICAN GOLD TRADE

I n medieval Africa there was a land so rich in gold that its ruler was rumored to tie his horse to a huge nugget of gold weighing more than 29 pounds (13 kg). This land was the early kingdom of Ghana, which was between the southern edge of the Sahara Desert and the northern reaches of the Senegal and Niger rivers. For many centuries Ghana was an important center for the trading of African gold.

The gold came from the west and south of the kingdom of Ghana. In some places pits were dug to mine it. In others gold dust sparkled in the beds of rivers and streams or in the sand along the seashore. The gold was taken by traders to market centers such as Djénné, Timbuktu, Gao, and Awdaghust. There it was exchanged, often for salt from the great salt mines near Taghaza, in the Sahara Desert. One Arab traveler who visited Awdaghust in the 11th century found a busy town with bright-colored cloth, brass jars and kettles, salt, dried fruits of all kinds, honey, and, of course, gold, all being traded in the bustling marketplace.

Across the desert

Some time during the first four centuries AD, camels were introduced into North Africa. They revolutionized travel and trade across the Sahara Desert. The Sahara is a huge expanse of arid sand and rock with few water holes, but a camel can travel for ten or more days without water, living off the liquid stored in its body. Using camels as pack animals allowed traders to cross the vast distances of the Sahara, and a thriving trade quickly developed.

A golden head belonging to the king of Ghana. The head probably is a portrait of an important enemy killed in battle.

THE LAND OF GOLD

Ghana was called "the land of gold" by an Arab historian. All gold nuggets found in Ghana were the property of the king, but ordinary people were permitted to keep gold dust. Another Arab traveler described the wealth of the royal court. The king's horses were covered in golden cloth, his slaves carried golden shields and swords, his dogs wore collars studded with gold and silver, and the king himself wore many rich golden ornaments.

14

The camels carried blocks of salt southward, in addition to luxury goods such as cotton and woolen cloth, spices and perfumes, beads made from glass, shell and stone, and brass and copper containers. On the return journey north, the camels carried their precious load of gold and ivory, too.

European interest

Much of the gold that crossed the Sahara was eventually sold to European merchants, and it was well known in Europe that it came overland from distant West Africa. In the 1400s the lure of African gold enticed the Portuguese to start exploring the coast of Africa by sea. In 1471 a merchant from Lisbon, Fernão Gomes, discovered a country so rich in gold that he named it "El Mina," meaning "The Mine." The people of this region, the Akan, were happy to trade with the Portuguese. The Europeans brought linen, belts, red caps, beads, and trinkets to exchange for gold dust and the golden ornaments worn by the Akan.

The Portuguese tried to keep their new source of gold a secret from other European countries, but they had no success. Soon ships from France, England, and Holland were sailing down the African coast in order to trade for gold. However, the attention of Europe was soon to turn elsewhere . . . across the Atlantic Ocean to the riches of the "New World."

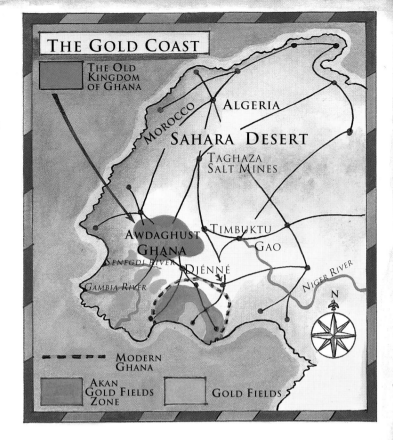

This map shows the main trade routes across the Sahara and the market centers mentioned in the text.

Golden jewelry from Ghana.

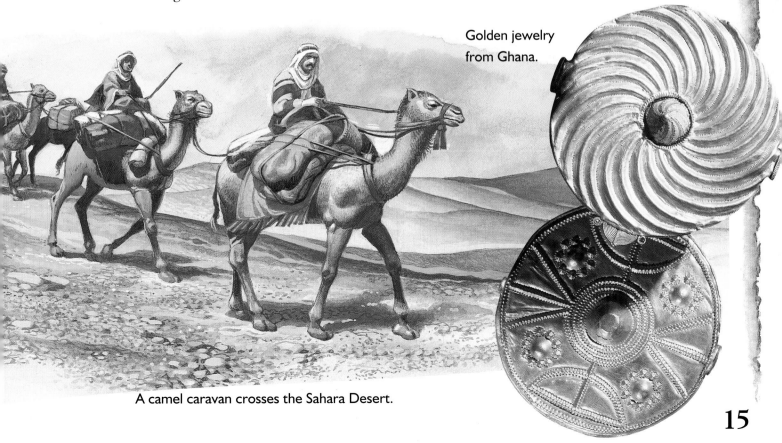

A camel caravan crosses the Sahara Desert.

GREED FOR GOLD

Portugal's exploration of Africa's "Gold Coast" led to a huge increase in the amount of gold pouring into Lisbon. Other European countries sent their own ships to try to trade for gold, but Portugal guarded its claim over the gold trade jealously.

The rulers of Spain were especially concerned about their neighbor's newfound wealth. But what could they do about it? Then, one day, a stranger came to the Spanish court with an extraordinary and exciting proposition.

The stranger was an Italian sailor called Christopher Columbus. He had lived for many years in Lisbon and had sailed along the coast of Africa under the Portuguese flag.

But Columbus's dreams took him far beyond the shores of Africa. He had heard tales of lands in the Far East that were said to be rich in silks, spices, and, most of all, gold. The overland trade routes to the East were long and dangerous. Columbus was convinced that there was another way to reach the fabulous countries of the East—since the world was round, he could get there by sailing west across the Atlantic Ocean.

Columbus presented his plan to the Portuguese king, but the Portuguese were too concerned with their African trade to listen to his crazy ideas. So Columbus decided to explain his intentions to King Ferdinand and Queen Isabella of Spain instead. It took him seven long years to convince them.

Sailing west to reach the East

Columbus sailed from Spain in August of 1492. But after more than a month at sea without any sign of land, the crews of his small fleet were beginning to doubt their captain's word. Then, on October 12, a lookout on one of the ships saw a hint of moonlight on distant cliffs. Maybe Columbus's ideas weren't so crazy after all!

Columbus spent several months exploring the lands he had found.

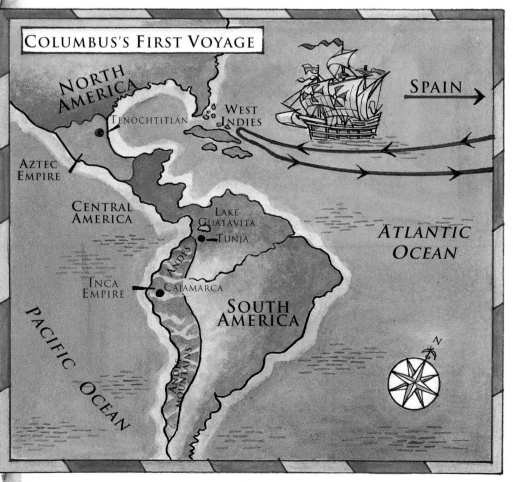

COLUMBUS'S FIRST VOYAGE

NORTH AMERICA

WEST INDIES

TENOCHTITLAN

AZTEC EMPIRE

CENTRAL AMERICA

LAKE GUATAVITA

TUNJA

ANDES

INCA EMPIRE

CAJAMARCA

SOUTH AMERICA

PACIFIC OCEAN

ANDES MOUNTAINS

SPAIN

ATLANTIC OCEAN

N

Columbus's first voyage to the New World and the extent of the Aztec and Inca empires before the Spanish invasion.

Columbus returns triumphantly to King Ferdinand and Queen Isabella of Spain, laden with exotic gifts from the New World.

He was convinced that he had reached the Far East, although we know today that he had actually journeyed to the islands in the Caribbean. There were many people living there at the time, and the Europeans were greeted with a mixture of fear and curiosity. They were also met by the sight of gold ornaments, which the local people seemed happy to barter for glass beads, small bells, and red cloth caps. In March of 1493, Columbus returned triumphantly to Spain, taking with him exotic plants and animals never before seen in Europe, such as pineapples, parrots, and the greatest treasure of all—gold.

But where is the gold?

Columbus made three further voyages to the New World. The first Spanish settlements were founded on the islands, and new crops such as sugarcane were introduced. But the quantity of gold was disappointing; there was certainly not an endless supply to ship back to Spain. Then, in 1519, an expedition of 11 ships left the island of Cuba to visit the mainland, which was still mostly unexplored by Europeans. The expedition was commanded by a Spanish soldier named Hernán Cortés. He was looking for slaves to work in the Spanish settlements, and for more gold. He stumbled upon the great civilization of the Aztecs, centered on present-day Mexico, ruled by the Emperor Moctezuma.

Columbus bartered with the local people for their gold ornaments.

THE FALL OF THE AZTECS

The Emperor Moctezuma (also known as "Montezuma") and Cortés met on November 8, 1519, just outside the capital of the Aztec Empire, Tenochtitlán. They exchanged necklaces made from gold and precious stones. Then, in procession, the Spaniards and the Aztecs entered the great city together.

Once inside Tenochtitlán, the Spanish soldiers lost little time in placing Moctezuma and his court under guard. Over the next two years, the Aztecs put up strong resistance to the Spanish invaders, but in 1521 the Aztec Empire was overthrown, and Cortés became the first governor of "New Spain."

Aztec wealth

The wealth of the defeated Aztec Empire was beyond the wildest dreams of the Spanish invaders. Some of the gifts given to Cortés included golden ornaments in the shapes of dogs, pumas, jaguars, and monkeys, as well as two round plates of gold and silver "as large as cartwheels." Most of the beautiful gold objects seized by the Spaniards were melted down to make them easier to bring back to Spain. The plunder of the New World had begun.

More Spanish adventurers

News of the wealth of New Spain traveled back to Europe. Many Spanish adventurers would soon try to make their fortunes in the New World. One of these was a soldier named Francisco Pizarro.

The Aztec emperor, Moctezuma, as portrayed by a European artist of the 16th century.

An Inca beaker, made from gold and decorated with human faces and frogs.

In 1532 Pizarro found himself in the great Inca Empire that stretched for 1,988 miles (3,200 km) down the west coast of South America. With his band of well-armed men, Pizarro led the way up the rough road that wound high into the Andes Mountains. At the town of Cajamarca, the Spaniards were met by the Inca emperor, Sapa Inca Atahualpa, and his attendants.

Like Moctezuma, Atahualpa welcomed the strangers with hospitality. But the Spaniards ambushed the unsuspecting Incas, killing the Sapa Inca's followers and kidnapping him. They locked him in one of the temples in Cajamarca and proceeded to loot the town and the tents of the Inca army. They collected all the gold, silver, and jewelry that they could find.

A ransom betrayed

When Atahualpa saw the Spaniards' greed for gold, he came up with a plan. He made a pledge that, in return for his freedom, one of the halls of the temple should be filled as high as he could reach with gold, and twice over with silver. Pizarro and his men could not believe their ears. They quickly agreed to the Sapa Inca's terms, but secretly they had little intention of ever setting him free. On Atahualpa's orders, gold and silver began pouring in from all corners of the empire. The Spanish watched in disbelief as huge sheets of gold that had been ripped from temple walls, finely worked statues, bowls and dishes, and ornaments and jewelry of all kinds were brought to Cajamarca.

Just as they had done in the Aztec Empire, the Spaniards melted down most of the gold and silver objects they seized and transported the metal in bars back to Spain. They put Atahualpa on trial and, on a pretense, executed him. Then they marched to the Inca capital, Cuzco, and captured it. The Inca Empire had fallen.

Piling up the gold for Atahualpa's ransom.

THE GOLDEN MAN

Many treasure hunters were not as fortunate as Cortés and Pizarro, and the lust for gold led people to believe some strange tales. One of the strangest was that of El Dorado—the "Golden Man"—which reached the ears of the Spanish as they explored South America in the 16th century. The rumor was based on truth, but it quickly grew to become a legend of untold wealth.

The story of El Dorado fascinated European explorers, and many became convinced that if there was a Golden Man there must also be a golden city, where the streets were paved with gold and the people were surrounded by unimaginable riches.

The search for El Dorado

One of the first expeditions to reach the lake was led by Gonzalo Jiménez de Quesada. He came upon the Chibcha city of Tunja, high in the mountain regions of the Andes. The city was full of thatched wooden houses, and from each house hung a thin sheet of beaten gold, swinging and tinkling lightly in the wind. Quesada and his men cut down the gold plates and ransacked the city for more golden loot. Then they were taken to Lake Guatavita. The ceremony of the Golden Man had been stopped many years before, but an old man told them what he could remember of it. The Spaniards could only look at the quiet waters of the lake and imagine what treasures lay in its depths.

A golden model showing the raft of El Dorado loaded with golden offerings.

The truth behind the legend

High up in the Andes Mountains, in what is now Colombia, lived a peaceful people called the Chibcha. In part of their territory was an unusual lake, perfectly round and surrounded by a steep rim, called Lake Guatavita.

When the Chibcha people elected a new leader, a ceremony was performed at the lake. This involved the new leader smearing his body with a sticky gum and then covering the gum with gold dust. Here was El Dorado—the Golden Man. He sat on a raft that was loaded with gold and emerald offerings and sailed to the middle of the lake, where he threw the offerings into the water.

Draining the lake

The obvious solution was to try to drain the lake, and the first attempt was made in 1544 by Quesada's brother. He organized teams to empty water out of the lake until, after three months' hard labor, the water level had fallen by about 9.8 feet (3 m). He found a few precious objects around the edge of the lake. A more serious attempt was made in 1578, when Antonio Sepúlveda ordered 8,000 local people to dig a channel through the rim surrounding the

RALEIGH'S DREAM

The English sailor Sir Walter Raleigh was one of those obsessed by the legend of the golden city of El Dorado. His first expedition to look for it was in 1595, when he promised Queen Elizabeth I of England that he would return laden with golden riches. He came back empty-handed. After her death he fell from favor and was imprisoned in the Tower of London. He was released in 1616 in order to set sail for South America, and once again he returned in disgrace. He was beheaded on a charge of high treason in 1618.

lake. Much of the water drained out, and Sepúlveda gathered up many golden offerings, including a huge emerald the size of an egg. However, when Sepúlveda commanded the channel to be deepened, disaster struck. The sides caved in, killing hundreds of diggers.

There have been other attempts to drain the lake, but no one has made their fortune from Lake Guatavita. Explorers continued to believe in the legend of the hidden wealth of El Dorado and continued to search for the "golden city." But their efforts were fruitless, and many perished in the attempt.

In 1578 the side of Lake Guatavita caved in after a channel was dug to drain the lake.

21

TREASURE FLEETS AND SEA DOGS

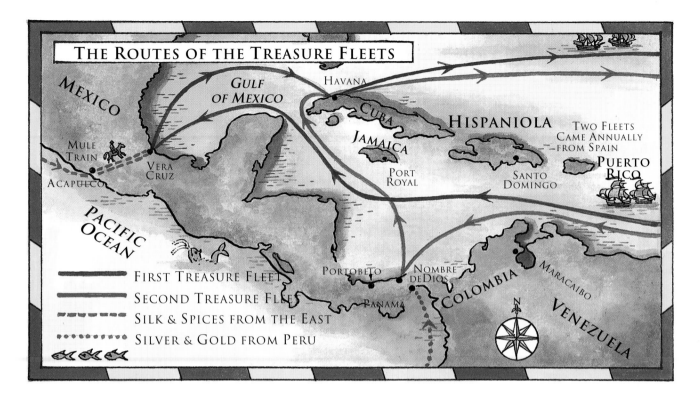

THE ROUTES OF THE TREASURE FLEETS

MEXICO

GULF OF MEXICO

HAVANA

CUBA

JAMAICA

HISPANIOLA

TWO FLEETS CAME ANNUALLY FROM SPAIN

PUERTO RICO

MULE TRAIN

VERA CRUZ

ACAPULCO

PORT ROYAL

SANTO DOMINGO

PACIFIC OCEAN

PORTOBELO

NOMBRE DE DIOS

PANAMA

COLOMBIA

MARACAIBO

VENEZUELA

N

———— FIRST TREASURE FLEET
———— SECOND TREASURE FLEET
– – – – SILK & SPICES FROM THE EAST
• • • • • SILVER & GOLD FROM PERU

The gold and silver plundered from Central and South America were to make Spain one of the richest nations in the world. But there was one problem with all this newfound wealth—it was on the far side of the Atlantic Ocean. Before Spain could make use of its American riches, the gold and silver had to be shipped back across the ocean, and the journey was full of dangers.

Like Portugal after its exploration of the African Gold Coast, Spain tried to stop ships from other European nations from entering the waters of its New World territories. Spain laid claim to all the land and sea to the west of an imaginary line running north to south, 298 miles (480 km) west of the Azores in the Atlantic Ocean. However, it was not long before foreign ships began to challenge Spain's rights in the Caribbean.

In 1537, French pirates invaded several Spanish settlements and attacked a Spanish fleet loaded with Inca treasure. They captured nine ships and made off with their cargoes of gold and silver. In 1543, France and Spain went to war, and the attacks in the Caribbean grew even more frequent.

The treasure fleets

Faced with an increasing number of assaults by French privateers, the Spaniards made greater efforts to protect the precious cargoes on board their ships as they sailed home to Spain. From the 1560s onward there were, in fact, two treasure fleets that traveled between Spain and the Caribbean. One of them left Spain in April and sailed to Vera Cruz on the mainland of New Spain (in modern Mexico). There the ships were packed with gold and silver from the fallen Aztec Empire, in addition to treasures from farther abroad. Spanish ships sailed regularly

PIRATE OR PRIVATEER?

What was the difference between a pirate and a privateer?
A pirate attacked ships of any nation in order to make a profit for himself and his crew. He was a criminal working outside the law of any country. A privateer sailed during times of war with a special letter from his government, called a "letter of marque," which gave him permission to attack ships belonging to his country's enemy. A privateer did not attack ships from his own, or other friendly, nations. Sir Francis Drake was an English privateer who attacked Spanish ships with the approval of Queen Elizabeth I.

between Acapulco (also in Mexico) on the west coast of New Spain and the Philippines, where they brought exquisite silks and valuable spices. The silks and spices were carried overland from Acapulco to Vera Cruz by mule train.

The second fleet sailed from Spain in August, bound for Nombre de Dios (in Panama) on the "Spanish Main." Inca gold and silver were transported by sea to the town of Panama and then taken by land to Nombre de Dios to be loaded onto the Spanish ships.

Each fleet was protected by two armed warships. The two fleets met in Havana (Cuba) at the beginning of each year to take on supplies before setting sail for Spain. The long journey home would be a perilous one.

Ships from the Spanish treasure fleet.

DUTCH PRIVATEERS

In 1628 a Dutch privateer named Piet Heyn captured the entire Spanish treasure fleet as it set off for Spain. Every ship was loaded with gold and silver, none of which reached the home country. The financial blow was terrible for Spain, but the loot helped to finance Dutch trade with Brazil for many years to come.

Gold and silver from the Aztec and Inca empires were melted down for use in coins, jewelry, and other objects.

Drake Takes His Revenge

One of the most famous of all the English privateers was Sir Francis Drake. In 1568 the young Drake had a narrow escape when he was forced to flee a Spanish attack near Vera Cruz. Drake claimed to have been tricked, and he was determined to take his revenge upon the Spaniards.

Drake left England in 1572 for Nombre de Dios, intending to raid the town. But the Spanish treasure fleet had departed only a few weeks earlier, and there was little in the town worth taking. Drake then set off overland, crossing the thin strip of land known as the Isthmus of Panama. On the west coast of Central America he became the first Englishman ever to set eyes on the Pacific Ocean.

Ambush!

Drake planned to attack one of the Spanish mule trains that carried gold and silver from the Inca mines across the Isthmus to Nombre de Dios. On the night of the ambush he ordered his men to lie in wait until he gave the order to attack. He could hear the tinkling of the bells as the mule train made its way down the steep, dusty track. But one of Drake's companions was drunk, and in his excitement,

Sir Francis Drake, one of the most famous of all the English privateers.

jumped up in full sight of the Spanish before Drake gave the order. The element of surprise was lost, and the mule train scattered in all directions.

Later Drake and his men had another opportunity to ambush a mule train, just outside Nombre de Dios. This time they managed to capture the mules and their precious treasure. Drake returned triumphantly to England with more than $31,000 (worth over $31 million today), mostly in the form of silver.

CAPTURED CHARTS

Gold and silver were not the only treasures taken by Drake from captured ships along the South American Pacific Coast. On board two Spanish vessels, he found charts showing the route used by the galleons that sailed from Acapulco to the Philippines. Drake knew that he could not return to England the same way that he had come—there were too many Spanish ships bent on revenge against him. So he used the charts to sail north, visiting the coast of California and then turning west to the Philippines to continue the long journey home.

Drake's ship, the *Golden Hind,* sails through the Strait of Magellan.

Drake and his men ambush the Spanish mule train.

The Golden Hind

Drake went on to make several more voyages. His most famous lasted three years and took him around the world. He sailed through the Strait of Magellan and then up the Pacific Coast of South America, raiding Spanish settlements as he went. Off the coast of Ecuador, he captured the Spanish treasure ship *Nuestra Señora de la Concepcíon* that was carrying 13 chests of coins and huge amounts of gold and silver. On that voyage Drake looted more treasure than he could cram into the holds of his ship, the *Golden Hind,* and once again he returned home victorious and won a hero's welcome from his queen.

PIRATES AND BUCCANEERS

As the 1600s dawned, Spain was still insisting upon its right to control all settlements and trade in "Spanish" America. But as time passed, more and more settlers and traders from other European countries poured in. Colonies were founded by the Dutch in Curaçao, by the English in Virginia and Bermuda, and by the French in Martinique and Guadeloupe. There was little the Spanish could do to prevent this.

The Spanish authorities did try to stop some of the illegal trading in their colonies. They knew that Dutch ships stopped at the small Spanish settlements on the northern coast of the island of Hispaniola in order to trade for supplies for the long journey home.

So they forced all the Spanish settlers in that region to leave their homes and move nearer to the island's capital, Santo Domingo, where the governor could keep an eye on them.

The "cow killers"

Unfortunately the Spanish authorities had not taken into account the other inhabitants of the wild country along the northern coast. These were the "cow killers," groups of men who lived by hunting the herds of cows and pigs that roamed the island. They lived rough lives, and they were a rough bunch! As the years passed, their numbers grew. Some were marooned on Hispaniola, some were escaped slaves or prisoners, others were religious refugees fleeing persecution in their own countries. The cow killers were happy to trade their meat and hides with passing ships in exchange for gunpowder, bullets, guns, brandy, rum, and other provisions.

These men were a lawless gang who were united only by their opposition to the Spanish. They became known as buccaneers.

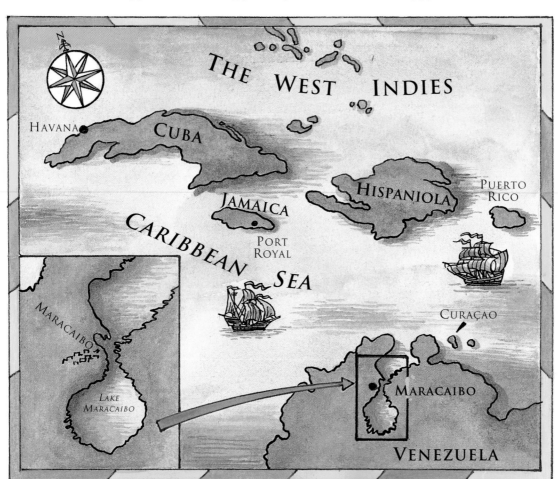

Buccaneer sites in the Caribbean.

Buccaneers attack a Spanish ship.

From boucan to buccaneer

Where did the name "buccaneer" come from? The buccaneers lived off meat, but in the tropical heat of the Caribbean a carcass would start to go bad in a matter of hours. From the local people of the island, the buccaneers learned how to cure meat in order to stop it from spoiling. They built a kind of barbecue and hung strips of meat over the fire. Once the meat was cured, it was called *boucan*. From this name, the men came to be called *boucaniers,* or buccaneers.

"No purchase, no pay"

The buccaneers traded with Dutch, French, or English ships, but if a Spanish ship was unlucky enough to sail too close to a hostile shore, the buccaneers would attack. If they captured the ship, they took it over. In this way groups of buccaneers built up small fleets that they used to make raiding voyages on Spanish settlements. The principle behind these trips was "no purchase, no pay." If no loot was taken, no one was paid. The buccaneers were interested only in plunder, and they soon became feared and hated throughout the Caribbean for their terrible violence and cruelty.

A buccaneer in typical dress.

BUCCANEER DRESS

The early buccaneers were savage by nature and savage in appearance. A buccaneer wore a loose jacket or tunic that was stained deep red by the blood of the animals he killed. His "trousers" were often simply a long strip of hide wound around the legs from knee to ankle—and very smelly! Around his waist a piece of hide acted as a belt. Pouches of gunpowder, bullets, knives, and a mosquito net for sleeping out hung from this belt. Shoes were made from pigskin tied around the feet and allowed to dry until it had molded to the shape of the feet.

Jamaica

In 1655, English troops captured Jamaica, and the island soon became an English colony. However, the new colony was constantly under threat from the Spanish, and England, like France, could not afford to keep a regular navy in the Caribbean to protect its settlements. Unwillingly, the governor of Jamaica saw the many advantages of using the buccaneer "army" to attack the Spaniards and protect English interests. Many buccaneers moved to the capital of Jamaica, Port Royal. One of these was to become the most famous of them all—Henry Morgan.

CAPTAIN HENRY MORGAN

Henry Morgan was born in Wales, and he first traveled to the Caribbean with the army that captured Jamaica. He stayed on the island and quickly joined up with the buccaneer forces in Port Royal. With the English governor's backing, Morgan commanded the buccaneer army that raided some of the best-defended Spanish settlements in the Caribbean, including Cuba and Portobelo. These raids were considered great successes. But when Morgan decided to attack Maracaibo, on the coast of Venezuela, the Spaniards had a surprise in store for him.

Morgan in Maracaibo

The entrance to Lake Maracaibo was a narrow channel overlooked by a Spanish fort. Undaunted, Morgan fought his way to the lake, and for the next few weeks the buccaneers raided and looted the towns around its shores. When Morgan decided that it was time to make a getaway, he sent a small ship to the mouth of the channel to see if the coast was clear. The news was not good. While Morgan and his men had been busy with their plunder, three Spanish warships had arrived, full of guns and troops. The buccaneers were caught in a trap.

The Spanish commander, Don Alonso del Campo y Espinosa, sent a message to Morgan. If he would surrender all the loot and release all the captives he had seized, he would be allowed to go free. In true buccaneer spirit, Morgan and his men decided to fight their way out rather than give up their hard-earned booty.

Captain Henry Morgan, the most daring of all the buccaneers.

Morgan's fleet sailed to the narrow entrance of Lake Maracaibo to meet the Spanish warships. Using gunpowder charges, the buccaneers made a fire ship that would sail beside the Spanish fleet and explode.

The fire ship

One of the buccaneers had an idea. Morgan had captured a ship in one of his raids around the lake—they could use this as a fire ship. The buccaneers filled the ship with palm leaves covered in tar. They laid charges of gunpowder beneath the palm leaves. Then, on the deck, they perched wooden posts topped with hats to make the Spaniards think that the ship was manned. Morgan's fleet sailed slowly toward the entrance of the channel, with the fire ship out in front.

The Spaniards suspected a plot, but by the time they realized what was going on, the burning fire ship was alongside their flagship. With a tremendous roar, the fire ship exploded, and soon the Spanish ship was also on fire and drifting toward the shore. In his haste to avoid the flames, the commander of one of the other ships sailed into shallow water and ran aground. The buccaneers captured the third ship, and Morgan triumphantly took it as his flagship. They had overwhelmed the Spanish warships—but they were not free yet.

BUCCANEER NAMES

When someone became a buccaneer, it was usual for him to take a false title. Here are some of the most famous buccaneer names:

★ Borgne-Fesse *(meaning "Half-Bottom," because he had half his bottom shot off by a cannonball!)*

★ L'Olonnais the Terrible *(who took his name from his hometown in France, Sables d'Olonne)*

★ Bartolemmeo the Portuguese

★ Rock Braziliano

★ Montbars the Exterminator

★ Red Legs Greaves *(an escaped prisoner from Scotland)*

★ Babord-Amure *(meaning "Port-Tack," because his nose had been smashed and pointed to port: the left side of a ship)*

The buccaneers' trick—hiding in the bottom of the canoes.

A cunning plan

Don Alonso was now installed in the fort. Morgan's ships would have to sail directly beneath its walls in order to reach open sea, and Don Alonso was determined that they should not escape. So Morgan thought up an ingenious plan.

From the fort, the Spaniards kept watch over the buccaneers. As evening approached, the lookouts saw canoes full of heavily armed buccaneers being paddled toward the shore. The canoes returned empty to the ships, then full once more to the shore. The lookouts ran to Don Alonso to report these strange movements. The buccaneers' plot was obvious—they were going to attack the fort from the other side.

Under cover of darkness

Immediately, Don Alonso ordered the heavy guns in the fort to be turned around to face the land. As darkness fell, he and his troops waited in expectation for the assault to come. Suddenly they heard the distant sound of a cannon firing, then again and again. Seven times the cannon roared, signaling to Don Alonso that Morgan had escaped once more. His fleet had slipped out through the channel under cover of darkness, and none of the Spaniards had noticed it going.

Of course, Morgan had played a cunning trick on Don Alonso. The canoes had gone to the shore full of men, but on the return journey the buccaneers had hidden in the bottom of the boats, out of sight of the Spaniards. Morgan returned to Port Royal on May 17, 1669, a rich and victorious man.

Missing treasure

The last great raid of Henry Morgan's buccaneering career was on the Spanish treasure town of Panama. By the time he had captured the well-defended town, most of the gold and silver from its churches and treasure houses had been removed and put on ships. Morgan's men nearly captured the Spanish ship, *La Santissima Trinidada*, that was carrying huge amounts of gold, silver, and jewels, but the buccaneers were too drunk to attack, and the prize escaped. Nevertheless, they did collect a huge amount of loot. But when the time came to divide the captured booty, the buccaneers were dismayed at the small size of their share. Surely some of the treasure was missing? Just as the buccaneers were beginning to get really angry, Morgan's ship was seen sailing away. Had he tricked his men? And had he buried some of the treasure during the journey back from Panama? No one knows.

A finely made golden cross set with precious gemstones and pearls. Morgan collected huge amounts of loot like this after his attack on Panama.

The destruction of Port Royal in 1692.

PORT ROYAL: THE BUCCANEERS' CAPITAL

Port Royal, in Jamaica, was the buccaneers' capital city, where Morgan and his men came to spend their ill-gotten wealth. It was once called the "wickedest city on Earth," and it was famous for its gambling dens, taverns, and wealth. In later life Morgan turned his back on his buccaneering career and became Lieutenant-Governor of Port Royal. He died in 1688. Four years later, on June 7, 1692, a huge earthquake and tidal wave swallowed up Port Royal. Overnight, the "wickedest city" was wiped off the face of the Earth.

THE FEARSOME BLACKBEARD

Blackbeard's real name was Edward Teach. He was a pirate with a frightening reputation, partly because of his fearlessness and partly because of his extraordinary appearance. He had a huge black beard that he twisted into long pigtails. Before attacking an enemy, he would throw a sling across his shoulders stuffed with pistols, and around his waist he wore a belt hung with daggers, pistols, and a cutlass. To complete the effect, he would tuck lighted fuses under his hat. Even to the bravest fighter he was a terrifying figure.

It was rumored that, some time before his death in 1718, Blackbeard buried a large treasure chest on Plum Island off the North American coast. In 1928 two fishermen claimed to have come across a large hole dug into a beach on the island. At the bottom of the hole they could see the imprint of a large chest. Had someone found Blackbeard's treasure? Again, no one knows.

Blackbeard's real name was Edward Teach. He terrified his enemies with his extraordinary appearance.

Walking the plank was one of many cruel punishments that pirates were said to inflict on their prisoners.

WILLIAM KIDD TRIES TO STRIKE A BARGAIN

Another mystery surrounds the pirate William Kidd. Kidd was an English merchant and sailor who set off in 1696 to search for pirates in the Indian and Atlantic oceans. This was a privateering voyage backed by the English government. For over a year, Kidd hunted for pirate ships without any success. Finally his crew turned mutinous. They had been recruited on the "no purchase, no pay" principle, so they knew that if they did not capture any ships they would earn no money.

Under pressure from his crew, Kidd decided to turn pirate himself. Instead of looking only for enemy ships, he would attack vessels from any country. His greatest prize was the *Quedah Merchant*, from which he looted gold bars and coins worth about $93,000. Kidd sailed the *Quedah Merchant* to the Caribbean, where he discovered that he was to be arrested for piracy. But before his arrest, he managed secretly to bury a large amount of the booty, possibly on Gardiner's Island in New York.

Kidd was put on trial in England and was sentenced to death for piracy. In desperation he tried to bargain for his life. He proposed to lead an expedition to recover his buried treasure. But the English government refused his offer, and he was hanged on May 23, 1701.

What happened to Kidd's treasure? It is likely that the loot was quickly discovered and dug up by other pirates, but this has not stopped people from searching many places to try to find it. Kidd's exploits also provided the inspiration for many pirate tales, including Robert Louis Stevenson's famous *Treasure Island*.

A map of Robert Louis Stevenson's treasure island.

A painting of Captain Kidd on board his ship, the *Adventure*.

PIRATE WORDS

There are many words and phrases associated with pirates and piracy. Here are a few of the best known:
- ★ cutlass: *a short sword with a curved blade*
- ★ doubloon: *a Spanish gold coin*
- ★ filibuster: *an adaption of the French* filibustier, *meaning a buccaneer*
- ★ freebooter: *another word for a buccaneer or pirate*
- ★ Jolly Roger: *the skull-and-crossbones flag flown by pirates*
- ★ pieces of eight: *the name given by pirates to silver Spanish coins found on treasure ships*
- ★ stinkpot: *a burning missile that gave off smoke, used by pirates when boarding a ship*

RUSHING FOR GOLD

One January morning in 1848, a man named James Marshall was examining the bed of a stream in California. A glint of something yellow caught his eye. It was a piece of gold, about half the size of a pea. Marshall's discovery sparked an era of gold madness. Here was a chance for ordinary people to go to the goldfields and make a claim, and they flocked from all over the world, lured by the prospect of "getting rich quick." However, as we shall see, Marshall and his partner, John Sutter, were not entirely happy about their amazing find.

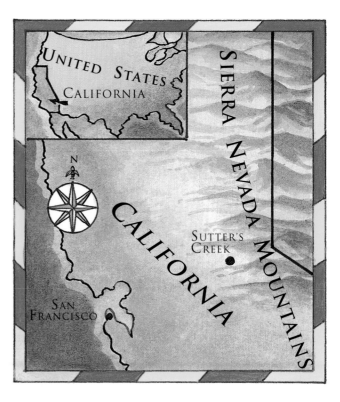

In 1848 gold was found in the Sierra Nevada Mountains in California. This discovery started the biggest gold rush in history.

John Sutter originally came from Switzerland, but he settled in the foothills of the Sierra Nevada Mountains in California, in 1839, and built a small estate that became known as Sutter's Fort. He and James Marshall teamed up to construct a sawmill, about 37 miles (60 km) from Sutter's Fort. They built it on a fast-flowing stream in order to use the power of the water to turn the mill wheel. But when the sawmill was completed, Marshall found that the water was too shallow to turn the wheel fast enough, so he ordered his men to dig out the bed of the stream to make it deeper. It was as he was inspecting their work that he made his important discovery.

Is it gold?

Marshall gathered several pieces of metal, then returned to the camp where his men were eating breakfast. The question in Marshall's mind was—is this gold? He knew that another mineral called iron pyrite looks like gold; in fact, its nickname is "fool's gold." So Marshall decided to do some simple experiments to test his find. First he hammered the "gold." It was soft and easily workable. Then he put a piece in the center of the campfire. It came out unchanged. Finally the camp cook dropped the gold into boiling water with a type of acid. Again, the gold was unchanged. Marshall saddled his horse and rode as fast as he could to tell Sutter the news.

ENTER LEVI STRAUSS

Some people came to California to find gold. Others made their fortunes by supplying the prospectors with all their basic needs—equipment, food, clothing. One man who made the journey from Germany to the western coast of America was Levi Strauss. He brought with him a type of cloth from which he made hard-wearing, practical trousers. He called them levis—and they are still known by this name today.

PANNING FOR GOLD

How did the prospectors find the gold? The simplest way was by using a flat dish called a "pan." This was filled with sand and gravel from the bottom of a river, together with some water. Then the prospector swilled the pan around in a circular motion, washing out the light sand and gravel while any gold remained behind, because it is very heavy. As you can imagine, panning was a long and back-breaking job.

Marshall shows Sutter the gold.

The secret is out

Marshall demanded an immediate, secret meeting with Sutter. In the privacy of Sutter's office, with the doors locked, Marshall showed his partner the gold. Neither of them was overjoyed about the find. Sutter didn't own the land on which the sawmill was built, and he knew that reports of gold would probably bring hordes of treasure seekers to the area. The two men decided to keep their find a secret at least until the work on the mill was finished. In the meantime, Sutter would try to secure ownership of the land. But any hopes of secrecy soon faded. Word leaked out and strangers began to pour into the area. So began the biggest gold rush in history.

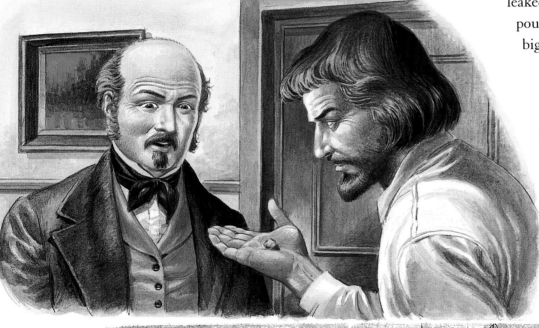

Marshall found gold in the stream running through this sawmill.

Gold for everyone

People came to California from all over America, and then from all over the world. A report in the *New York Daily Tribune* stated: "The only machinery necessary in the new gold mines of California is a stout pair of arms, a shovel and a tin pan." There was gold for everyone—shopkeepers, farmers, soldiers, sailors, professors, or judges. By the end of 1849, the population of California (not including Native Americans) had risen from 26,000 to more than 115,000, and still people kept coming.

Poverty and ruin

What happened to John Sutter and James Marshall? As the discoverers of the gold, they should have become rich men. But as he had foreseen, Sutter's land was overrun by prospectors and his estate was ruined. He died a poor man in 1880. James Marshall turned to drink and also died a pauper in 1885.

HARGRAVES'S STORY

One prospector who traveled to the gold fields of California was Edward Hargraves. He was an Englishman who had lived most of his life in Australia. Hargraves didn't have much luck in California, but as he was panning in the foothills of the Sierra Nevada Mountains, he began to notice something strange. The mountainous Californian scenery reminded him of the landscape back in Australia, particularly around the Blue Mountains just west of Sydney. If there was gold in mountains like these in California, why not in Australia, too?

Hargraves returned to Australia in 1851. He went directly to the Blue Mountains and soon panned enough gold to convince himself that he had gotten lucky. He rode back to Sydney and informed the authorities of his find. With this news Hargraves started the second great gold rush.

Gold in Australia

The first people to come to the Blue Mountains were disappointed with what they found. It was winter and the rains were falling, turning the dirt roads into

GOLD RUSH WORDS

★ blanket: *the layer of surface rock in which gold was embedded in the gold fields in South Africa*
★ cradle: *a wooden box used to sift for gold*
★ color: *a shout of "Color!" meant that a prospector had found gold—anything from a few flakes to a nugget*
★ forty-niner: *someone who travelled to California in the gold rush of 1849*
★ fossicker: *an Australian gold hunter*

seas of mud and drenching the prospectors as they worked. Many people gave up and struggled home, cursing Hargraves.

But Hargraves's good name was saved by a spectacular discovery near the town of Bathurst, when a huge chunk of gold, weighing more than 60 pounds (27 km), was uncovered. Another prospector dug down just over 3.2 feet (1 m) and found gold "so thickly sprinkled that it looked like a jeweler's shop." Others pulled up plants and found nuggets of gold clinging to the roots. And so the gold madness continued.

A lucky prospector. Bernhardt Holtermann, with the huge nugget of gold he found during the Australian gold rush. The nugget was named after him and made him a rich man.

Gold mining in the Blue Mountains of Australia.

GOLD IN SOUTH AFRICA

In 1886 a gold find was reported on a farm in the Transvaal region of South Africa. There was a small gold rush, but it quickly became obvious that this was no place for lone prospectors with their pans. Where the gold lay on the surface, it was embedded in hard rock. But most of it was in rich seams, called reefs, deep underground. Only large companies could afford the expensive equipment to dig deep enough to reach the gold. To this day the South African goldfields remain some of the richest in the world.

Drilling for gold deep in a South African gold mine.

THE LAST GOLD RUSH

For the last part of the gold-rush story, we travel back to the most northwestern region of America. It was one find in August of 1896 that sparked this gold rush. The news of gold, lots of gold, in the small Klondike Creek in the Yukon Territory of Canada encouraged prospectors from all over the world to travel there. Many had only the vaguest idea of where the Yukon Territory was or how they might get there, and few could have known about the terrible conditions they would encounter in their search for gold.

The Klondike trail

The first problem was getting to the Klondike. Many routes were tried, but one of the most popular was the trail from the town of Skagway, on the Alaskan coast, through the Chilkoot Pass. This pass was more than 3,280 feet (1,000 m) above sea level, too steep for horses to climb, and covered in snow throughout the year. At the top of the pass lay the border between Alaska and Canada. The Canadian authorities had laid down strict rules about the amount of food and equipment to be carried by the prospectors. They were worried about people starving to death during the long march ahead. So prospectors each had to take enough supplies for a year—too much to carry in one trip. They were forced to struggle many times up the steep, narrow path to the summit of the pass, until they had carried all their equipment to the top. It took some prospectors nearly three months to move everything.

To Dawson City

Once over the pass and into the Yukon Territory, the prospectors still had more than 600 miles (900 km) to travel before they reached the Klondike. Many went by boat down the Yukon River, through the raging Whitehorse Rapids. This was possible only between the months of May and October, when the river was not frozen over. Eventually those hardy prospectors who had not given up and turned back found themselves in Dawson City, the main meeting place and mining camp of the Klondike.

Mining in the Klondike

The harsh climate in the Klondike made mining for gold no easy task. In the short, hot summer, the prospectors were plagued by mosquitoes as they panned in the streams for gold dust. During the long, bitterly cold Arctic winter, the streams froze over and no mining was possible. Very few Klondike prospectors made their fortunes from the gold they found.

The main street of Dawson City in 1899, the height of the Klondike gold rush.

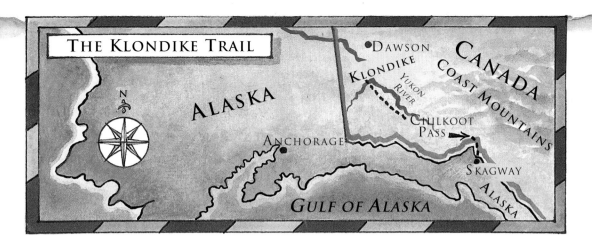

DAWSON
Klondike
CANADA
COAST MOUNTAINS
YUKON RIVER
CHILKOOT PASS
ALASKA
ANCHORAGE
SKAGWAY
ALASKA
GULF OF ALASKA
N

The route to the Klondike across the Chilkoot Pass.

Big companies move in

By the summer of 1899, the Klondike gold rush was over. The big companies moved in and took over from the small prospectors. Between 1899 and 1904, these companies mined over $100 million in gold from the Klondike. Today gold is still mined in this remote region, but its importance has been overshadowed by the discovery in Alaska of another precious resource—oil.

A continuous stream of prospectors struggles up the steep path to the top of the Chilkoot Pass.

PANNING IN THE TAVERNS

Whenever prospectors in the Klondike got lucky, they went to Dawson City to celebrate, often in the taverns. The prospectors carried their precious gold dust in small bags, called "pokes." As they bragged about their finds and showed off their pokes as proof of their worth, some of the fine dust would find its way into the sawdust spread on the floor of the tavern. Many tavern owners soon realized there was a small fortune to be had from their own floors and employed boys to pan the sawdust. One boy sifted more than $270 worth of gold from the floor of a tavern!

UNSOLVED MYSTERIES

There are many tales of lost or hidden treasure: treasure ships sunk beneath the waves, oak chests full of gold and silver buried by pirates, jewelry concealed during times of war, priceless golden artifacts placed in tombs. Here are just a few of the stories about lost treasures of the world, particularly the mysterious tales concerning the pirate treasure of Cocos Island and the strange money pit on Oak Island.

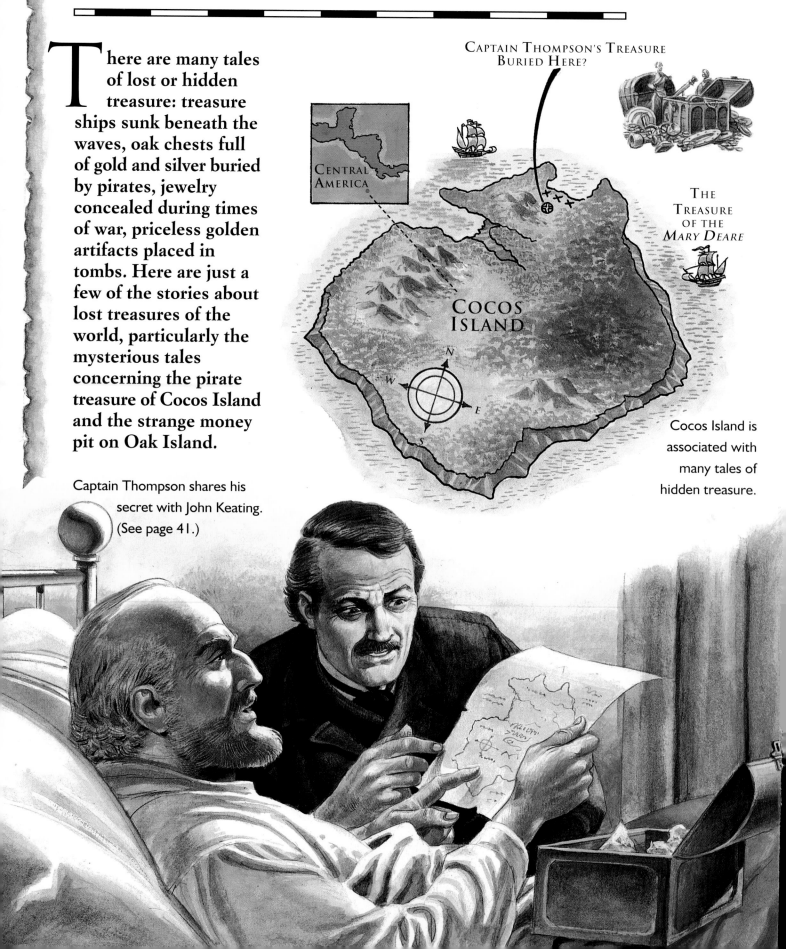

CAPTAIN THOMPSON'S TREASURE BURIED HERE?

CENTRAL AMERICA

THE TREASURE OF THE *MARY DEARE*

COCOS ISLAND

Cocos Island is associated with many tales of hidden treasure.

Captain Thompson shares his secret with John Keating.
(See page 41.)

Cocos is an island in the Pacific Ocean, about 311 miles (500 km) southwest of Costa Rica. It is roughly 3.7 miles (6 km) wide and 5.5 miles (9 km) long, and it is covered in dense tropical jungle. This small island was used as a pirate hideaway throughout the 17th and 18th centuries, and it is associated with many stories of pirates and their hidden treasure.

CAPTAIN THOMPSON AND THE *MARY DEARE*

The most famous of all the stories about Cocos starts in the capital of Peru, Lima. Ever since Pizarro rode into the Inca Empire and tricked Atahualpa (see pages 18–19), Peru had been a Spanish colony. But in 1823 the revolutionary leader Simón Bolívar was advancing with his army on Lima in order to free the country from Spanish rule. As the army drew near, the Spanish authorities quickly made plans to protect the wealth of the city.

The Spaniards packed up their treasure and took it to the neighboring port of Callao. To their dismay, the only ship there was the *Mary Deare,* commanded by a Scottish captain, William Thompson. The Spaniards had no choice—they were forced to entrust their precious treasure to Captain Thompson.

An unbelievable sight

The sailors on the *Mary Deare* couldn't believe their eyes as they loaded the valuable cargo into the ship's hold. Gold and silver statues, candlesticks, and plates were all thickly encrusted with precious jewels. The *Mary Deare* sailed with strict instructions from the Spanish authorities: Thompson was to stay near to Lima and wait to see if the city was captured. If it was not, he was to return the treasure. If it was captured, he was to deliver the treasure to the Spanish town of Panama.

However, the thought of the dazzling hoard lying below the decks was too much for Thompson and his crew. They murdered the Spanish guards on-board ship and threw their bodies overboard. Then they sailed to Cocos Island, where they hid the treasure in a cave.

A dirty deed discovered

Unfortunately for Captain Thompson and his crew, their dirty deed was already discovered. The bodies of the murdered guards had washed ashore and had been recognized. A Spanish warship captured the *Mary Deare*, and all the crew except for Thompson were hanged. The Spaniards took Thompson to Cocos in order to force him to reveal the hiding place of the treasure, but he escaped, and the Spanish eventually gave up the search.

Thompson was rescued from Cocos, but he was never able to raise enough money to return there to reclaim the loot. Just before his death, he shared the secret of its location with another sailor, John Keating. Keating did manage to travel to Cocos, and it is possible that he found at least part of the treasure. Since then, many people have searched the island for the rest of it, but with little success. It seems that much of Captain Thompson's ill-gotten booty must still lie undiscovered somewhere on Cocos Island.

A treasure chest from the 15th century designed with a sturdy lock to keep its contents safe.

THE MYSTERIOUS MONEY PIT

Oak Island is one of many small islands in Mahone Bay, Nova Scotia, on the eastern coast of Canada. The story of Oak Island starts in 1795 when three boys were exploring the eastern end of the island. In a clearing they came across a tree from which hung a block and tackle (these are used to lift heavy objects). Beneath this equipment was a slight dip in the ground. Someone had obviously been digging and had used the block and tackle to lower or lift something heavy. The boys knew all the rumors about pirates on Oak Island. Was this their chance of finding pirate treasure?

Digging for treasure

The boys decided to dig. They went home and returned to the island with shovels and a pick. They soon found themselves inside a well-built shaft. About 3.2 feet (1 m) down they removed a layer of flagstones, then 6.4 feet (2 m) deeper there was a layer of oak logs. They dug until the shaft was about 33 feet (10 m) deep. At this point the boys realized that they would need help to dig down any farther.

In 1804 work started once more on the mysterious pit. The diggers came upon layer after layer laid across the pit, made from charcoal, oak logs covered in putty, and large quantities of coconut fiber. They also found a stone with a message in code carved on it. The message was later translated as: "Forty feet (12 m) below $3.1 million are buried."

Three boys find a mysterious block and tackle.

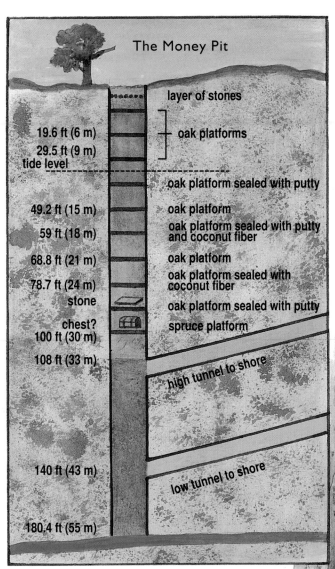

The Money Pit

- layer of stones
- oak platforms

19.6 ft (6 m)
29.5 ft (9 m)
tide level

- oak platform sealed with putty

49.2 ft (15 m) — oak platform

59 ft (18 m) — oak platform sealed with putty and coconut fiber

68.8 ft (21 m) — oak platform

78.7 ft (24 m) — oak platform sealed with coconut fiber

stone — oak platform sealed with putty

chest? — spruce platform
100 ft (30 m)

108 ft (33 m)

high tunnel to shore

140 ft (43 m)

low tunnel to shore

180.4 ft (55 m)

A cross section of the different layers of the money pit on Oak Island.

When the shaft was 98.4 feet (30 m) deep, the diggers thought they could detect a large wooden object at the bottom. A chest perhaps? It was late on a Saturday evening, and the workers decided to leave the final discovery until Monday morning. It was to be a decision they would regret. When they returned on Monday, they found the pit flooded with water.

The mystery deepens

Over the years many more expeditions went to Oak Island to try to uncover the secret of the pit. Many people tried to drain it, but they had little success. Then someone discovered that an elaborate series of drains led to a beach nearby. This was the source of the water; the pit filled up at every high tide. More shafts were sunk alongside the original pit until the whole eastern end of the island was devastated, with shafts and excavations everywhere. None of the diggers ever made any money out of Oak Island, and the mystery of what is buried in the pit, and who buried it there, remains as deep as ever.

Kidd's maps

One theory about the pit links Captain Kidd (see page 33) with Oak Island. Kidd left behind various clues concerning the whereabouts of his buried loot. The most famous of these "clues" are four maps, hidden in old chests that probably belonged to him. The chests were bought by a 20th-century collector named Hubert Palmer. Experts say that the writing on the maps matches that of the pirate. Could these maps show where Kidd buried the treasure from the *Quedah Merchant*? And could the island on the maps be Oak Island?

Captain Kidd buries his treasure.

LE VASSEUR'S CODE

On July 7, 1730, Olivier Le Vasseur was hanged for piracy. As he stepped forward on the scaffold, Le Vasseur threw a piece of paper into the crowd, shouting, "My treasures to the person who can find them!" On the paper was a message written in code. Many people have tried to break the code. One man spent more than 20 years looking for the pirate's buried treasure in the Seychelles, islands in the Indian Ocean. The mystery remains unsolved, however, and Le Vasseur's message is still puzzling treasure hunters the world over.

GLOSSARY

archaeology The study of human history by examining material remains such as sites of ancient cities, burial places, etc.

Aztec Empire In the 15th and 16th centuries, the Aztecs ruled a great empire in Central America, located in present-day Mexico, until the arrival of the Spanish invader, Cortés, in 1519.

brigand A robber or bandit, especially one who operates in a mountainous area.

buccaneer A pirate in the Caribbean in the 16th and 17th centuries.

caravan In the desert, a group of people traveling together, often with camels.

corroded The result of a chemical reaction that causes metal, such as iron, to rust.

fool's gold Iron pyrite, a mineral that looks like gold.

Inca Empire The Inca people ruled a huge empire in South America, based in modern Peru, for about 100 years, until the invasion of the Spanish in 1532.

letter of marque A document that gave a privateer permission to attack ships belonging to enemy nations.

maroon To abandon someone, often on an isolated island.

New Spain The lands claimed by Spain in Central America, Mexico, and the Caribbean.

New World The name given by Europeans to America after Columbus's voyage of 1492.

nugget A lump of something, often gold.

pirate A criminal, working outside the law of any country, who attacks and loots ships.

poke The small bag in which a prospector in North America often carried gold dust.

privateer Someone who attacked enemy ships with the backing of his government.

prospector Someone who searches for gold.

reef The word used in South Africa to describe a layer of gold embedded in rock.

Sapa Inca The title given to the emperor of the Incas.

Spanish Main The name often given in the 16th and 17th centuries to the northern coast of South America between Guyana and Panama.

tarnish The result of a chemical reaction that causes silver to discolor.

Ur The ancient civilization of Sumer in southern Mesopotamia (the land that lay between the Tigris and Euphrates rivers).

FURTHER READING

Colby, C. B. *The World's Best Lost Treasure Stories.* Sterling, 1992

Deem, James M. *How to Hunt Buried Treasure.* Houghton Mifflin, 1992

Donnelly, Judy. *True-Life Treasure Hunts* (Step into Reading Books: Step Four). Random Books for Young Readers, 1993

Gennings, S. *The Atocha Treasure.* (Great Adventure Series). Rourke Corporation, 1998

Gibbons, Gail. *Sunken Treasure* HarperCollins Children's Books, 1990

Green, Harriet H. and Martin, Sue G. *Treasure Hunts.* Good Apple, 1983

Homer, Larona. *Blackbeard the Pirate and Other Stories of the Pine Barrens.* Mid Atlantic, 1987

Lazo, Caroline E. *Missing Treasure* (Incredible Histories Series). Dorling Kindersley, 1994

Lye, Keith. *Spotlight on Gold* (Spotlight on Resources Series). Rourke Corporation, 1988

Marsh, Carole. *Avast, Ye Slobs! The Book of Silly Pirate Trivia.* Gallopade Publishing Group, 1994

Meltzer, Milton. *Gold: The True Story of Why People Search for It, Mine It, Trade It, Fight for It, Mint It, Display It, Steal It, and Kill for It.* HarperCollins Children's Books, 1993

Nesbit, Edith. *Story of the Treasure Seekers.* (Classics Series). Puffin Books, 1987

Platt, Richard. *Pirate.* Dorling Kindersley, 1995

Russell, William. *Gold and Silver.* Rourke Corporation, 1994

Shuter, Jane. *Exquemelin and the Pirates of the Caribbean* (History Eyewitness Series). Raintree Steck-Vaughn, 1995

Wright, Rachel. *Pirates.* Watts, 1991

INDEX